T0065375

THE GOLDEN YEARS

Growing Older But Not Old

*Life Lessons about
Aging Gracefully*

TRUEY ANNE STERNEMAN

WESTBOW
PRESS®
A DIVISION OF THOMAS NELSON
& ZONDERVAN

WestBow Press books may be ordered through booksellers or by contacting:

WestBow Press
A Division of Thomas Nelson & Zondervan
1663 Liberty Drive
Bloomington, IN 47403
www.westbowpress.com
844-714-3454

ISBN: 978-1-6642-0674-8 (sc)
ISBN: 978-1-6642-0675-5 (hc)
ISBN: 978-1-6642-0676-2 (e)

Library of Congress Control Number: 2020918494

Print information available on the last page.

WestBow Press rev. date: 11/16/2020

CHOICES for the Golden Years Growing Older but Not Old

Lessons:

In this little study on growing older,
I would like to credit my mother,
Truey Johnston-Cooper,
who never grew old although she was 101
when she finished her life journey.

Also, thanks to my fellow travelers who have
taught me so much on this journey
through the golden years.

ENDORSEMENTS FOR THE GOLDEN YEARS

Anne Sterneman shares wisdom from her years of joyful living in the Lord, lovingly and skillfully directing her readers' hearts to the truth of God's Word to aging with grace and purpose. Although written with the "golden years" in mind, all ages will benefit greatly from the wisdom and joy that flow from Anne's pen. For those who desire to follow Scripture's call to apply their hearts unto wisdom and to leave a godly legacy, this book is a must read!

Diane Eley

Bible Study Fellowship Teaching Leader, Indianapolis, IN

Author Truey Anne Sterneman presents a thoughtful, practical and comforting message about "the golden years." She presents a biblically based study format which chapter by chapter reinforces her observations about how to sustain healthy perspectives, attitudes and activities as someone progresses through this special period of life. Positive outlooks remedy ingrown fears. Anne's commitment to focus upon others, to sustain intentional prayer practices and her commitment to God's Word form the foundation for healthy golden years. Anyone who reads the content of this book and takes it to heart will find great comfort and value to the golden years of life.

Dr. Daniel L. Tipton
Pastor of the Daybreak Church, Etna, Ohio, former General Superintendent of the Churches of Christ in Christian Union

Your book is fantastic! You beautifully weave biblical lessons, stories, great quotes, targeted exhortations, and personal accounts into a great fabric. It should be required reading for anyone turning 65 years!

Dr. Richard Smith
Retired missionary and pastor

INTRODUCTION

This book was written to help us through our aging years. Each lesson is a compilation of stories and personal growth ideas with an emphasis on prayer and living as good stewards of the gifts God has given us.

After the introductory chapter, the subsequent chapters are based on the acronym CHOICES, emphasizing the importance of the choices we make throughout our life journey.

This small book could be used as a group study on aging. There are action plan notes placed after the first section of every lesson. At the end of the Bible hero section of each chapter, there is a "Keeping on action" segment with suggestions on how we can bless others, even in our golden years.

WHY DID GOD MAKE ME?

Tonight I sit quietly and think over past years.

Many thoughts come to mind of

the cheers and the tears,

Of a person once young and now growing old.

When life's books are opened, how

will my story be told?

God's Word clearly teaches that he had a plan;

He chose my arrival and into which clan.

What design for my life did my gracious God see

When he set out to make the one to be me?

Time left may be short – days fly by so fast.

When I come to life's end, and to Eternity pass,

How will he greet me on that glorious day,

When I stand by his throne, what will God say?

I long and I pray for these words to be true –

"Dear child of mine, I'm so glad I made you."

- Truey Anne Sterneman

LESSON 1

Introduction to the Golden Years and
the Model Given by Abraham's Life

> He will also keep you firm to the
> end, so that you will be
> blameless on the day of our Lord Jesus Christ.
> God is faithful, who has called you into
> fellowship with his Son, Jesus Christ our Lord.
>
> **1 Corinthians 1:8-9**

Experts tell us the keys to aging gracefully include accepting changes and finding meaningful activities. Sooner or later, we have to face it: no matter how determined we have been, we come face-to-face to that wall that says a different season of our life has arrived.

The changes may have come slowly, sometimes imperceptibly, but they still came, and we are now on the brink of what will inevitably be the last part of our life journey. But don't despair! My mom used to say that "Age is mind over matter. If you don't mind, it doesn't matter." She imparted such wisdom all her life until she went home to heaven at 101 years of age. Billy Graham put it well when he said, "When granted many years of life, growing old in age is natural, but growing old with grace is a choice."

God has always given mankind a choice. The choice that we face now is simple: Will we get older, or will we get old? That choice will determine how our life journey will finish.

When Adam and Eve lived in the garden of Eden, God gave them the ability to choose for themselves. When the serpent, that wily old devil, approached Eve with the question, "Did God really say . . . ?" He gave her an option to choose to obey what God had expressly commanded or to act in disobedience to God's will. We know now that Eve chose the wrong option and then led

Adam to go along with her. Mankind has suffered from that bad choice ever since.

From the time we are born until the time we leave this earth, choices are the biggest factors in our life journey. As we look at studying how to age gracefully, we will be looking at our choices, both the choices we have already made and the choices we have yet to make.

So, here we are, right at the golden years of life reflecting on our life story up to now. We look at old picture albums and go through ancient scrapbooks. We take side trips down memory lane and visit old friends and family, memorializing those who have gone on ahead. We read senior blogs such as "seventy candles" about thriving and realize that's us! As lady time advances, the truth hits – golden years, we're here.

We think of how quickly our life has flown and wonder what people will remember about us when we have finished our days on earth. God has favored those who reach the golden years with a great gift. A wise person once said, "Do not regret growing older. It's a privilege denied to many." My mom's spin was, "I'd rather be over the hill than under it." We are so blessed that God has let us live so long. And when we are called to leave, how do we choose our life story to read? What do we want on our epitaphs?

It's a fact of life that everyone has a story.
And though some may have much more glory,
The facts remain, we're all the same.
We're born, we grow, and we come to our end.
It's our CHOICES that determine our lives' dividend.

- Truey Anne Sterneman

Someone once made a sign that read:

"You are unique, just like everyone else"

Now that is a true saying. Everyone is unique. The life story you are writing has no double – in the whole wide world! Your story is unique, just like you.

Abraham Lincoln said in the opening lines of his famous Gettysburg Address that "all men are created equal." Yes, we all have the same moral worth, but there the equality seems to end. We are equal but not all the same. We all have different abilities and talents, and as we grow and mature, changes emerge, and our personal uniqueness sets in. Ethnicity, family background, societal position, and the surrounding culture are just a few of the elements blending together to distinguish each person who comes into this world.

Some come with a silver spoon, and some come with no spoon at all. Our development shapes to fit our environment. We each begin our own unique life journey. So, Mr. Lincoln, we may be created equal, but we are all different. To each is given the opportunity to choose. We can accept what we are and grow and change according to God's plan or we can run our own show. In this lesson, we will see how one Bible hero chose to live.

Action plan for group study

On a sticky note have each person write a sentence or two about Abraham. Have these posted on a bulletin board and have someone read the collective thoughts about the man whose epitaph reads:

Here lies father Abraham
He was GOD's friend

Abraham, the Man Who Chose to Follow God's Plan

Abraham began life in a pagan culture. Joshua 24:2 tells us that Abraham was an idol worshipper. But he made a stellar life choice: he turned his life over to God and became known as God's friend (II Chronicles 20:7; Isaiah 41:8; James 2:23). Abraham made other good choices, as well. He could have said "no" when God gave such huge orders, such as: "Pack up your family and leave all you have ever known behind and no, I am not telling you where you're going, just go." Later, God asked Abraham to give him his most precious possession, his beloved son. And that was not all, God said that Abraham was to sacrifice the boy himself. And Abraham obeyed. Whatever God asked for, Abraham gave. No matter how difficult the command was, Abraham obeyed! He chose well, and God loved him.

In Genesis chapters 12 to 25, God asked big things of Abraham and again Abraham said, yes. In Genesis 12:2-3, God made a seven-fold promise to Abraham. God promised to be with him; to protect him; to be Abraham's strength; to answer him, to provide for him; to give him peace; and to always love him. In Genesis 12:5-9, God gave the promise of land. And in Genesis 15:1-5, God promised Abraham a son and told him he would be the "father of a great nation."

For the most part, Abraham made good choices but sometimes he listened to the wrong advice as recorded in Genesis 16:1-3. From that side trip, Abraham became a father at eighty-six with Hagar, the slave woman who gave him Ishmael, his first son. This boy was not the son

God had promised but the choice of impatience. (And God's people are feeling the repercussions to this day). Genesis 17:17-22 tells us that when Abraham was ninety-nine God promised him that he would bless Ishmael but that Abraham and Sarah would have a son, the son God had promised so long ago. Genesis 21:1-8 records that when Abraham was one hundred years old Sarah gave birth to Isaac. She was merely ninety years of age!

Abraham had great faith and he was a man of prayer. He pled with God to spare the city of Sodom where his nephew Lot lived. Chapters 18-19 record that part of Abraham's story and the punishment for the sin of that place. In Genesis 22 is the account of Abraham passing God's supreme test of obedience to give back Isaac. Genesis 22:16 tells us that God was so pleased with the level of Abraham's commitment to obey that he promised that Abraham's descendants would greatly increase and that through Abraham's offspring, *all* the nations on earth would be blessed. This was the reward for Abraham's choice to love and obey God.

After Abraham had done all that God had planned

for him to do, God took him to his eternal reward. Genesis 25:7-8 records that Abraham was 175 years old when he died. Abraham made good choices and he lived to tell his little twin grandsons about his friend, God. I can only imagine the joy he had sitting around the fire in the evening regaling those little guys with his great stories. What a life story Abraham lived!

Think about your own life story. Use the story card at the end of this book to help you fill in the blanks. How has your life gone? How are you living now? How will you finish? What daily choices are you making? Ask God to help you make the right choices.

Keeping on action:

We sometimes hear people say, "Just keep on keeping on." Keeping on, according to the typical dictionary definition, means to persist in doing something. As we approach our golden years, we realize that for all of our life, we have been impacted by good and evil. When we put our trust in God and our faith in Jesus Christ, our actions change, and we begin to pursue the good: God's plan for our lives. This plan does not end until God calls us home to heaven. Paul the apostle put it well in Philippians 3:14 which says, "I press on toward the goal to win the prize for which God has called me heavenward in Christ Jesus."

So, the good word is, just keep on keeping on!

Keeping on action deed: Call a troubled friend. Don't pry, just visit, listen, and offer prayer.

LESSON 2

·◇◆◇·

Caring and Complete in God's Love: Observing the Lives of Ruth and Naomi

> **The righteous cry out, and the Lord hears them;**
>
> **he delivers them from all their troubles.**
>
> **The Lord is close to the brokenhearted**
>
> **and saves those who are crushed in spirit.**
>
> **Psalm 34.17-18**

Phenomenal advances in medicine have caused people to live far beyond the proverbial three score and ten years of life as predicted by the psalmist in Psalm 90:10. In today's world, it seems that many are living quite a bit longer. People today reach retirement age with the joyous prospect of many happy days ahead of them. The freedom from "clock domination" seems to be very special. And for a while, retirement is great! This is the life! Or is it?

Of course, there are those who are able to settle into the "coping with old age" routine and that is okay, but many feel they have much more life to live and more love to give. They soon tire of the "too much time on my hands" syndrome and before long they begin to explore the endless opportunities for living out their golden years. Those whose faith is in God begin to search for ways to advance his kingdom. They find fulfillment in volunteering and helping others. Caring about the needs of others becomes a way of life. Life is good. Then the inevitable changes come as the decades pile up. Physical difficulties seem to come closer together, and our new way of life is jeopardized in ways unimaginable.

We seem to have no control over things which happen to us. Current events and catastrophes can easily cause fear and anxiety. Most of the time we cannot anticipate or be prepared for these new challenges. On 9/11, who could have imagined the horrific events that would take place that day?

Although we cannot prepare for the problems which may be ahead, we know that God is there with us. His word reminds us that he cares for us. The message in Psalm 34:17-18 is clear: The LORD does hear his children's prayers. He is near to the broken hearted and he does lift up those whose spirits are crushed.

God wants to care for us and make us complete. He desires our trust and faith. He reminds us "I am here for you, I care, you are complete in me. I know what you need."

As the time of this writing, our nation, even the world, is held in the clutches of a huge pandemic. Life has virtually come to a standstill for many as we are ordered to shelter in place. No one is supposed to leave home unless they are essential workers or are going out for necessities. For most of us, life was going on as usual and suddenly, everything changed. A "new normal" descended upon us and changed our lives – perhaps forever.

Many acts of kindness and caring have sprung from this event in our history. People are looking out for one another. Some are calling on senior citizens to offer help. Life has swung into an easier style, the "mad rush of life" has abated somewhat and we are discovering new joys. Parents are home-schooling their children, using school-originated lessons plans and finding delight in this task. One mother of a first grader remarked that she had no idea what a clever and thoughtful child her son was becoming. On the flipside are parents eager for schools to reopen. They have found that teaching is not their "thing." Sadly, chaos and frustration may become the norm during the school hours.

This pandemic was something that we could not control. Like so many other life events, it just happened, and we were left to find ways to cope with its challenges.

Often as senior adults, we find ourselves in similar predicaments. We are going on as usual and suddenly, our life takes a dramatic turn, and we find ourselves facing painful events that will shape our days to come. It may be the death of a spouse, a bad medical report, or retirement, which for some equates to being "put out to pasture."

With these changes, our life journey takes a new path. Those who are able may volunteer their services to others less mobile. Some may even become caregivers. Some will give and find joy in visiting, calling or even texting friends who are homebound or in retirement centers. Taking time for hospitality is a great way to show God's love to others. Pray for ways to avoid slipping into the easy rut of just plodding along without any plan. Get involved in a small group or a neighborhood Bible Study, even if you must start it yourself. Great joy can come from the fellowship and sharing.

The Bible hero study at the end of this lesson will give us a look into the lives of two women who reacted differently to major life changes. We will see how, in the end, both were made complete and whole again.

A big factor in facing each day is our mental attitude. We all smile at the old story of the woman who was asked "Did you wake up grumpy again this morning?" to which she replied, "No, I let him sleep in." That is funny but it packs a potent punch. Sometimes we are the ones to get out on the wrong side of the bed! A daily antidote to that problem is to decide upon waking that this is a good day to be happy and serve the Lord.

One older lady began to lean heavily on the joy of the Lord. She put signs about her house that read: "Today I Choose Joy." Even on the days she was not feeling the greatest, these signs put a smile on her face and a spring in her step.

Although we may be widowed or far from family, there is a lot of joyous living to be found, and good choices will enrich our lives and bring care and completeness to those around us.

Above all else, get involved in prayer. It is the direct line to heaven! Make a special prayer place in your home. Write to those on the "front lines." Ask about special needs or requests so that when we pray, we can be specific. Too many times, we pray "God bless the missionaries." God likes specificity in prayers! William Carey, known as the father of modern missions, gave much credit to his sister Polly for any victories he won for Christ in India. Even though paralyzed and bedridden for fifty-two years, Polly daily lifted up each need and request she received from William.

The importance of prayer was greatly impressed upon me as noted in the following personal story.

Years ago, when my husband was in church administration, we were privileged to attend a pastoral retreat at the Cove in North Carolina. The experience was wondrous, and we learned so much. However, one story impacted me more than all else. The speaker spoke about prayer and the illustration she gave was my big take-away. It remains dear to my memory even today.

It concerned a worldly-wise businesswoman who had recently moved into a new area. Searching through the newspaper for something to do, she spotted an ad for a women's retreat and made arrangements to attend, unaware that it was a Christian women's event.

While she was there, she found Christ as her Savior. Speaking to one of the keynote speakers, she expressed her joy at coming into the family of God. His response was: "Well, someone has been praying for you," "Oh no," she returned, "I don't hang out with praying people." He continued, "Yes, someone has been praying for you." However, Mrs. Business Lady felt in her heart that prayers for her would have been quite impossible.

Soon after she returned home, her doorbell rang. It was a shy little lady bearing a loaf of bread. She explained that she was a back-fence neighbor and had been too busy to visit sooner. But, she added, "I have been praying for you."

We may never know what our prayers will accomplish. We are just told to be faithful in prayer.

Action plan for group study

On a sticky note, write a sentence or two about the Bible story of Ruth and her mother-in-law, Naomi. What do we know about these women? Did God care about their problems? Put notes on the bulletin board and have someone read the collective words about a special woman who chose to follow the true God and how this changed her mother-in-law's life and her own.

Ruth and Naomi, A Story of Caring and Completeness

Throughout the ages, people have set goals and dreamed dreams. God made us that way. Although the biblical account of Ruth and Naomi is over 3,000 years old, it still remains the standard as a beautiful example of setting new goals and achieving new dreams by following God's plan and enjoying his caring love.

This book of Ruth, which contains only four chapters, a brief twenty minute read, is nestled between Judges and 1 Samuel. Even though it is a tiny book, it contains a wealth of information about the way God works for those who put their trust in him. And even those who did not, like Naomi. As we read the biblical account of these two women, we see that although they suffered much from the brutal realities of life, God cared for them and made them complete.

In the first chapter of Ruth, we find that Naomi was a good wife and mother when she and husband Elimelech set out from their Judean homeland with their two sons and worldly goods. Their decision to move was caused by a dreadful famine which had ravished their country and they were seeking a new start in Moab, a pagan city about 60 miles from Jerusalem.

Life in Moab was good for about ten years. The boys grew up and married young Moabite women, which may have caused distress for Naomi. However, there was food to eat and Naomi was surrounded by family members who cared for her.

But we never know what tomorrow will bring. Tragedy struck this contented family and just five short verses into the narrative, Naomi found herself both widowed and childless. This was a time of deep grief for Naomi and she decided to return home to Bethlehem. Her two daughters-in-law pledged to go with her. It is here, in the rest of the story that we see caring love in action.

Ruth 1:6-22 tells of Naomi's pleas for her daughters-in-law to return to their Moabite families. She puts forth the reasons, benefits and wisdom of her appeal. Orpah agrees and returns to her people and that is the last we hear of her.

Ruth, on the other hand, makes a different choice and clings to her mother-in-law, accepting Naomi's God and country and vowing to stay with her. This choice to care for her husband's grief-stricken mother is truly a beautiful expression of sacrificial love.

In the second chapter of the book of Ruth, we meet Boaz and witness his kindness to the two bereft widows. Chapter three gives the account of Naomi's plan to take care of Ruth by securing a husband for her. Chapter four portrays the amazing end to this delightful story: Ruth and Boaz are married, Naomi becomes a grandmother, and Ruth, because of her loving choices, finds happiness and completeness as Boaz's wife and takes her place in the annals of Jewish history for all time and eternity.

Only God could have planned and orchestrated such a plot. The story ends with Grandma Naomi in her new completeness, caring for her precious grandson, Obed. And Ruth, the one who chose to leave behind all she held dear to become a caregiver, became great-grandmother to the illustrious King David, ultimately entering into the lineage of our Lord Jesus Christ. That is a great family tree and a beautiful life journey.

THOUGHT QUESTIONS:

1. How did Naomi react to her losses? Was her reaction typical of that day or do we see the same behavior today?
2. How could the choices have been different?
3. What motivated Ruth to go with Naomi? Was this an easy decision for Ruth . . . remember, she had suffered major life changes as well.
4. Did Ruth's decision bring about personal satisfaction?
5. How did the choices made by Ruth and Naomi influence the outcome of the story?

Keeping on action:

The selfless love that Ruth demonstrated is a great life example – she kept on even when faced with difficult decisions. In these golden years, it may become easy to dwell on our own personal problems and frailties, yet, God has work for us to do even now. Keep your heart open and prayerfully seek ways to show God's love and care to the multitude of the needy ones around us and even those in faraway places. Keep on caring and praying for others.

LESSON 3

*Hopeful and Helping with a
Look at the Life of Rahab*

> For I know the plans I have for
> you, declares the LORD,
> plans to prosper you and not to harm you,
> plans to give you hope and a future.
> Then you will call on me and
> come and pray to me,
> and I will listen to you. You will
> seek me and find me
> when you seek me with all your heart.
>
> ***Jeremiah 29:11-13***

Why Am I Here?

Sometimes while listening, it seems I hear
A question ringing loud and clear;
"Of all the people in all the ages
What am I writing on my life pages?"

Dear Lord above, Creator of love,
You know about me and my family tree.

You brought me to earth, You planned my birth.
Now please help me to choose that I might not miss
Your will for my life in times such as this.

Help me to understand Jeremiah 29
Verses 11 through 13 – may they be mine.
Like Ruth and Rahab, may I be true
To the things You've planned for me to do.

- Truey Anne Sterneman

Have you ever turned philosopher and wondered why
you were put here on earth? What did God have in mind

when he created you? In our younger days, we all had big dreams and lofty ideas. What man cannot remember dreaming of being a fireman when he grew up? Or, what little girl did not dream of becoming a mother or even a nurse to help people? Dreams and goals are good. Dreams are like plans in process. Even for senior citizens, they give us a positive perspective. In dreams we can give thought to what we want to yet accomplish and how to make it happen. If we stop dreaming, life may become boring and tedious.

God had a plan when he made you. He has plans which will carry you through life. Even with the physical limitations that come with aging, to know that God is in control is an amazing gift for the golden years. We are his hands. We are his helpers. He has plans for us to share the hope that brings salvation and peace to the world.

Happy is the person who has come to terms with who he or she is and takes pleasure in the "me-ness" of God's pattern for their life. Remember, when God created you, he had a plan! He gave you the right personality and temperament to carry out that plan. He brought you to earth at just the right time period and in just the right place. A heart turned to God seeks and follows that plan. God hears the cry of a seeking heart.

When we were on a mission trip to India, it was our privilege to meet a young man training for Christian service. His story was a marvelous example of God's love. Lombardo was a Dalit, or from the untouchable caste of the Hindu religion. He told of having a deep desire to know God. This hunger became so great that he went to the temple to call upon God to see if he was real. He told of three different occasions when he went to the temple and called out, "God, if you're real, show me!" The first two times, he was met by silence, but on his third visit, he told of seeing a great light. He heard a voice from the light saying, "I am the way, the truth and the life."

But Lombardo did not understand the meaning of those words. Upon leaving the temple, he spotted a small pamphlet on the walkway. The message on the front was: I am the Way, the Truth and the Life. On the reverse side was an address. When Lombardo visited the address, he was led to Christ. Then he went to the seminary to prepare for a ministry to his village to share the gospel. God hears our prayers.

Even if we think we are done for, God gives hope. Just ask him. It may be that in all your life, you have never trusted Jesus as Savior as Lombardo did. It is a wonderful thing and never too late to be saved from eternal punishment. Jesus told Nicodemus in the biblical record of John 3:16 that new birth is imperative for reaching heaven. You can do that by asking forgiveness for sin, inviting Jesus into your heart and by putting him in the driver's seat of your life. It is as simple as that, and when you make that choice, tell everybody. This is great news!

We sometimes look around and wish that we could have been born in another age. We may think that life would be easier if only we had this or that commodity or disposition. Or, we think things would go better for us if we had been born with different physical attributes or if we were smarter. Maybe we wish we could have come in a different birth order or if we were more assertive, etc. On the other hand, we can choose to accept how God made us and let him do his work through us.

Every person born is patterned by God for the challenges that lay ahead on the journey of life. Some of us get diverted by the rabbit trails of wrong choices. Who among us would not like to go back in time and relive some of our history with the wisdom we have acquired at experience university!

Bill Bright's wonderful book, *Finishing Well*, is a masterpiece at revealing God's grace for one's final years. It tells of choices which may both help the reader and give hope. Bill Bright lived an incredible life of service for God. He began Crusade for Christ (now Cru) for ministry on university campuses. He also produced the film, *Jesus*, a powerful evangelistic tool used around the world to bring people to Christ. Added to the list of his accomplishments is the little booklet "Four Spiritual Laws," which he wrote to help people find faith in Christ. The first spiritual law is that "God loves you and has a wonderful plan for your life." Yes, even now in our senior years, we can live for God and bring glory to his kingdom.

Action plan for group study

On a sticky note, write what you know about the story of Rahab. Who was she and what did she do? Does our past define our future? Can we change – even in our senior years. Have these notes posted and shared.

Rahab, the Helper who Found the Hope of Heaven

A beautiful story of God's help and hope comes out of the second chapter of Judges. In this biblical record we are introduced to the story of a helper who needed hope. Francine Rivers described this woman, Rahab, "as a woman with a past to whom God gave a future." The story that Francine Rivers wove around Rahab's life is beautifully told in the novella Unashamed (Tyndale 2000).

Rahab was an innkeeper who added to her income by prostitution. Joshua, God's man to succeed Moses, sent two spies to Jericho to get the lay of the land. How they met up with Rehab is not recounted in the biblical record. They may have gone to her inn because that is where they could pick up the reconnaissance information they needed. We are not given the complete story, just the bare bones. We do know that Rahab helped the spies by hiding them and helping them to escape.

It was her belief that the wicked city of Jericho would be destroyed, and she was hoping for deliverance for herself and her family. The arrangement was that a scarlet cord would be placed in her window. When this seemingly impenetrable city was brought low, God's army would see the cord and bring Rahab and her family to safety before Jericho was destroyed.

Rahab was a helper placed in a strategic position by God. She chose to follow God's plan and brought about deliverance for herself and her people. James 2:2, Matthew 1:4-5 and Luke 3:32 all give references of God's blessing on her life. She later married Salmon, one of the spies. It was a joyful Rahab, with her forgiven past, who gave birth to Boaz, thereby entering into the lineage of Jesus Christ, the Messiah and Savior of the world. For Boaz was the father of Obed, who was the father of Jesse, who was the father of King David through whom all the world was blessed.

THOUGHT QUESTIONS:

1. Why do you think Rahab helped the spies?
2. What similarities do you see between the lives of Rahab and Lombardo?
3. Is it easy to break free from one's beginnings?
4. How do you think Rahab and Lombardo found peace with God?

Keeping on action:

Because of her work in prostitution, Rahab was a woman most people would avoid. She had lived a life of shame. But God had a plan for her and when given the chance, Rahab made the choice that marked her eternal destiny. In helping the spies, she found the hope of heaven, and we will meet her someday.

Look for those you can help. God will probably not send spies, but there are others who need help. A kind word or a prayer for some lonely person can change a life forever.

LESSON 4

✦◆✦◆✦

Obedient and Optimistic: Admiring Mary, the Mother of Jesus

> **Observe what the LORD your God requires:**
>
> **walk in obedience to him,**
>
> **and keep his decrees and commands,**
>
> **his laws and regulations, as written**
>
> **in the Law of Moses.**
>
> **Do this so that you may prosper in**
>
> **all you do and wherever you go.**
>
> **1 Kings 2:3**

Among the emails I receive, I found a funny picture of two dogs, one was a large dog with mud half-way up his legs and the other, a much smaller dog with mud up to his neck. The caption was, "How deep the mud is depends on who you ask." The tagline for the picture parable was: "We all go through the same stuff differently." Very true of life experiences! It is often our faith that determines our reactions.

The apostle Paul asserted with conviction in Philippians 4:13 "I can do all things through Christ who gives me strength." Paul had found the key for facing life fearlessly. His creed works for us – at any age. God will give us an optimistic outlook if we give him our steadfast obedience, no matter what comes along.

A friend, Carol Sinsel, was just getting into retirement from a teaching at a private college in West Virginia. She had served there for several years as chair of the Health, Human Performance and Recreation Department. Retirement was good, or it was until she received a devastating medical report from her doctor. She was diagnosed with adenocarcinoma, which is lung cancer. This eventually spread to her bones and brain. The story she tells of this precarious wilderness journey is truly an account of amazing optimism and obedience.

When I asked Carol how she first reacted to this news, she stated that it was a "win-win" situation . . . God would heal her on earth or give her the ultimate heavenly healing. She was not depressed but felt completely at peace.

Along with husband Steve, Carol has witnessed some incredible miracles, both physically and financially, as a result of prayer. The couple truly needed financial miracles when medication bills skyrocketed to thousands of dollars each month. Physical miracles have graced her recovery as well. Carol says, "I had cancer in six different places in my brain... and the doctors were amazed that I didn't show signs of slurred speech, seizures, etc." other unimaginable miracles have filled her story with awesome wonderment at God's power and love.

Her summary of the ordeal is, "God had the plan, we just needed to get out of the way." This experience which included countless trips to the hospital, has given Carol many opportunities to share her faith with staff and medical personnel.

When I reflect on Carol's story, I wonder how I might have reacted in similar circumstances. It is good that our life journey is planned by God to fit each one personally. He has the plan.

Benjamin Franklin claimed that he grabbed the newspaper upon waking each morning and then he checked the obituary page. "If my name is not on it," he said, "I get up." We smile at his humor. But waking each morning in our golden years is truly a gift. Sometimes, it is a good thing just to lay quietly for a moment and thank God for the day and then ask for his help to get through it.

Some days it may be more difficult to focus on God's blessings. The choice of how we start the day pretty much sets the tone for what follows. We may encounter days when our body determines how the day will be spent. Physical pain and confusion may define the order of the day. God knows all about our troubles and he will help us through. It is our job to be obedient and look with optimism on what God has planned.

Thomas Edison tried many ways to create the lightbulb. He discovered thousands of prototypes that did not work, but these were not labeled failures. To him, they were learning experiments of what would not work. He just kept seeking one that would work. Optimism helps people cope with unfortunate news. May God give us optimism in our golden years and obedience as we age.

Action plan for group study

Distribute sticky notes and ask each person to write a sentence describing Mary, the mother of Jesus. Have these posted and shared.

Mary, the Mother of Jesus: A Life of Optimistic Obedience

One year, when my husband was conference superintendent for the Free Methodist Church, we were able to give each pastoral couple a lovely ceramic nativity set. Carl and Lillian served in our most southern church and occasionally cared for their young grandson. Lillian once shared this treasured story of obedience and how a child's outlook may differ from ours.

She had carefully arranged this special Christmas

display on the coffee table in the living room, telling her grandson that he could "look but not touch." Sometime later she went into the room and to her dismay, the nativity set had been completely rearranged into a circular order, only Jesus was not in the circle. He was set alone in the center of the display. She reprimanded Jeremy and put the figures back into the more traditional setting warning him of dire consequences should he touch the set again. Upon completing her tasks, she returned to where the little boy was playing. To her chagrin, she found the figures arranged once again to Jeremy's design. Scolding him, she asked why he had disobeyed again. "Grandma," he explained tearfully, "I wanted Jesus in the middle so everyone could see him."

When Jesus is in the middle of even our golden years, we can see God's plan much more clearly.

We are all familiar with the beautiful Christmas narrative. A story showing God's love to people by sending his only son to provide salvation to those who would believe. Most of us could tell in detail about the angel's visit to Mary and later appearing to Joseph as well. We know all about the trip to Bethlehem and the sad news of "no room in the inn." We can recall the shepherds' wonder and later we realize that the wisemen's gifts were given to provide funds for the flight to Egypt, the trip which prevented Satan from thwarting God's plan of salvation.

All these pieces of the Christmas story we know well and cherish. But when we look deeper into the events surrounding Jesus' birth, we find there is so much more! When we consider in depth the part Mary was given, we are amazed at her optimism and unswerving obedience. We can only imagine the feelings she must have experienced.

Mary was a simple Jewish girl, perhaps in her early teens when the angel, Gabriel, came to her with God's message. We marvel at Mary's response and her submissive spirit. Luke 1:38 gives us an unsurpassed illustration of obedience by recording her words: "I am the Lord's servant. May your word to me be fulfilled."

Her submission to God's plan put her in a dicey position which came at great personal expense. Her obedience would affect her reputation, Joseph's reaction, and later, her beloved son would be taken from her and murdered by an unbelieving and disobedient mob.

God chose Mary because of her courageous and obedient spirit and he chose well. Mary must have been amazed that she was the one chosen to be mother of the Christ child. Later in Luke 2, we read that Mary thought deeply about what was happening in her life. She recalled what the angel had told her, what Joseph discovered, and the witness of her cousin Elizabeth. The shepherds also confirmed that she had been highly honored. Mary treasured up all these things and pondered them in her heart.

Because of her obedient and optimistic spirit, Mary had the joy of seeing Jesus grow and develop. Although she did not fully understand his mission, she gave him all the guidance she knew to give. Luke 2:50- 51 relates that even though Mary did not understand him, she treasured his deeds and words in her mother's heart. Luke 2:52 shows that she was undoubtedly a good mom, because Jesus grew "in favor with God and with man."

Only God knew the sufferings that lay ahead for this little handmaiden of the Lord. It is good to know that after the horrific events of Jesus' death, God privileged her to be at the tomb when the resurrection was discovered. What a gift! After that, Mary became part of the New Testament church and continued to serve God and others. In Acts 1:14 we see Mary still doing her part and praying along with the disciples and other believers. Mary is a prime example of optimism and obedience.

THOUGHT QUESTIONS:

1. Of all the possible choices, why do you think Mary was picked to be Jesus' mother?
2. Is it likely that Mary knew what would happen when her pregnancy was discovered?
3. What do you see as the most important aspect of Mary's story?
4. Is it always easy to be obedient and optimistic?

Keeping on action:

God will give us opportunities to serve, maybe taking a meal or a special treat to a shut-in. God keeps the records and he knows the deeds we do and the words we say. May we have the courage to say and do that which will bless many people.

LESSON 5

Inner Peace and Inspiration as Modeled by King David

> **Peace I leave with you; my peace I give you.**
>
> **I do not give to you as the world gives.**
>
> **Do not let your hearts be troubled**
>
> **and do not be afraid.**
>
> **John 14:27**

After his paralyzing accident, actor Christopher Reeves, best remembered as Superman, chose to be hopeful even with the dreadful prognosis of paralysis from the neck down. He worked hard with what he had and any movement he attained gave him joy and hope.

What an outlook for our golden years! No, we will

not get back our former youth, but we can focus on what we still have. Remember, "it ain't over til it's over."

Cleaning off some old bookshelves recently, I found an old volume I had forgotten was in my library. It was a first edition of a book written by Fanny Crosby and the title was: *Fanny Crosby's Life Story by Herself.* It was published by EveryWhere Publishing Company in 1903, twelve years before the beloved hymnwriter passed into glory at age ninety-five. Blinded at six weeks by medical error, Fanny Crosby refused to feel sorry for her plight. When she was eight years old, she wrote, "Oh, what a happy soul I am, although I cannot see! I am resolved that in this world contented I will be. How many blessings I enjoy that other people don't. To weep and sigh because I'm blind, I cannot and I won't!"

Fanny Crosby lived to serve God and exhibited an inner peace that inspired all who knew her. Although she played harp, piano, guitar and other instruments, she is best remembered for the music she wrote. Many beloved hymns such as "Blessed Assurance," "To God Be the Glory," and "Safe in the Arms of Jesus" came from her gifted pen. These are only a few of the over eight thousand hymns bearing her name.

Much has been written about peace. One researcher found over fifty thousand books devoted to that sought-after state of emotional serenity. Peace gives us happiness and joy when we are living for God.

The secret to Mrs. Fanny Crosby Van Alstyne's inner peace is that she learned to use the talents God gave her, instead of mourning what she lacked. Fanny Crosby was married to Mr. Alexander Van Alstyne in 1858 but continued to use her maiden name at his request as she was already known by that name. He, too, was a blind musician and they shared forty-four years of marriage until his death in 1902.

Years ago, while a student at the Missionary Training Institute in Nyack, New York (now Nyack College), I needed to earn extra money for school and living expenses. God blessed me with a job working for Mr. & Mrs. Ernest Luleich. This couple owned and operated Luleich's Bakery, a place of wonderful baked goodies.

I did not work at the bakery but spent my weekends cleaning their lovely home on Sickles Avenue.

Dorothy Luleich was truly an amazing and godly woman. Her life story contained several twists and turns that might have defeated a less determined person. However, when she put her faith in God, her life took a totally different path. She became a source of inspiration for all who knew her. Our Saturday morning visits were the highlight of my week. She would come home about ten in the morning with a bakery delight and summon me to the kitchen where we would share what God had been up to in our lives during the past week. In her gentle way, she counseled and advised me, making a lasting contribution to my life journey. And not only to me, but countless other students were recipients of her caring prayers.

Behind her desk at the bakery was a large board with names and pictures of many students. Some of these students were current employees. Others had already graduated and were in churches or were global workers serving the Lord. Dorothy regularly took these students to the throne of heaven. Only glory will reveal the effects of the prayer seeds she planted.

This dear lady could have lived life for herself, but she chose to live in such a way that even with problems and disappointments, her life became productive and brought joy to many and glory to God, She learned to dance in the rain storms of life. People like Dorothy Luleich do not wait for the rain to stop! They dance and spread peace and inspiration to all they meet.

John Dunlop made some insightful observations in his book on aging *Finishing Well.* His advice was to choose to serve others and enjoy close friendships. Following his simple rules brings inspirations to us and joy to others. Reach out and make new friends now. Invite someone in for coffee and chat. You will be glad you did.

Our golden years give us time to invest in others. We have much to pass on to the next generation about what we have learned. Take time to share. Tell about your family tree. Inspire the ones who follow after you as they reflect upon your life journey.

Action plan for group study

On a sticky note, write your favorite
inspirational verse from the Psalms. King
David wrote many of these! Share and discuss
these verses shared with the group.

David, the King: A Model of Inner Peace and Inspiration

David was just a shepherd lad when Samuel was sent to the house of Jesse to anoint a new king for God's people. Jesse had eight sons, seven of whom were paraded before the aged prophet, but God said, "No" to each one. David, the little brother, was then summoned from the field where he had been tending the sheep. Although he was just a boy, he was the one chosen by God to be Israel's next king. He was later known as a man after God's own heart.

David's "rags to riches" story, written mainly in 1 and 2 Samuel, is a wondrous account of how God loved this courageous man. The story of his bravery in taking on the nine-foot giant, Goliath, is one that inspires many. But it is David's inner peace, found so often in his writings that endear him to us in these golden years. Historians credit David with at least seventy-five of the Psalms. The one which is probably the most beloved is Psalm 23. Here David recorded the words of comfort and inner peace which were the most important elements of his life.

The LORD is my shepherd, I lack nothing.

He makes me lie down in green pastures,

he leads me beside quiet waters, he refreshes my soul.

He guides me along the right paths for his name's sake.

Even though I walk through the darkest valley,

I will fear no evil, for you are with me;

your rod and your staff, they comfort me.

You prepare a table before me in

the presence of my enemies.

You anoint my head with oil; my cup overflows.

Surely your goodness and love will

follow me all the days of my life,

and I will dwell in the house of the LORD forever.

This psalm pretty much summarizes David's life. He had followed God to the still waters. He had been restored by God's loving care. The valley of the shadow of death was a real place in Jerusalem, and David knew all about the traumatic events which took place there. Yet, he could pen the above lines because of his personal relationship with God. He was able to hand his troubles over to the shepherd Lord, who cared for him.

Later on in his life as king, David fought many battles. He knew all about armor and armor bearers. But his protection came mainly from God, with whom he regularly communicated through obedience and prayer. His inner peace came from knowing that God was with him and that God had a special place in heaven ready for him.

Some days, it is comforting to reflect, as David did, upon what is ahead of us, to think about the time when our earthly journey is finished, and we dwell in the house of the Lord forever. David was ready for that life because he had committed his life to God. 1 Kings 2:2-3 records David's special words to Solomon, the next king. "I am about to go the way of all the earth," he said. "So be strong, act like a man, and observe what the Lord your God requires: Walk in obedience to him, and keep his decrees and commands, his laws and regulations, as written in the Law of Moses. Do this so that you may prosper in all you do and wherever you go." In these, his final words, David again reveals the secret of his inner peace and inspiration: Do what the Lord God tells you. Walk in his ways. And he will help you.

Jesus shared about the life in the hereafter with his words recorded in John 14:2-3 "My Father's house has many rooms; if that were not so, would I have told you that I am going there to prepare a place for you? And if I go and prepare a place for you, I will come back and take you to be with me that you also may be where I am."

Great words of comfort for our aging days! We can be greatly encouraged in these days of hurts and aches by the fact that one day we will take up our residence in the house of the Lord!

THOUGHT QUESTIONS:

1. Why do you think David was the one chosen from all of Jesse's eight sons?

2. In what way would a shepherd's life appeal to you?

3. In Isaiah 26:3, we read, "You will keep in perfect peace those whose minds are steadfast, because they trust in you." How do you think Isaiah's words reflect David's life?

4. How can we be sure we will see David some day?

Keeping on action:

God had a special plan for David's life. David found favor with God because he obeyed him. This brought hard times to David, but he pressed on in obedience. It is never too late to give God our obedience. Then we will know the inner peace David knew and we can inspire others. Pray that God will give you someone to inspire today.

LESSON 6

Confident and Content:
Witnessing Paul's Experiences

I am not saying this because I am in need,
for I have learned to be content whatever the
circumstances. I know what it is to be in need,
and I know what it is to have plenty. I have
learned the secret of being content in any and
every situation, whether well fed or hungry,
whether living in plenty or in want. I can do
all this through him who gives me strength.

Philippians 4:11-13

Several years back, a story was told about an unforgettable airplane trip. The weather was a little "iffy" and the pilot had come over the loudspeaker informing passengers of some upcoming turbulence. All were required to fasten their seatbelts. The storm broke and the dark skies were lit up by flashes of lightening as the plane was buffeted about by strong winds. Some passengers were apprehensive about reaching their destinations; it was really that bad. All were afraid and concerned. All except one little girl. She was sitting calmly reading a book. She seemed not to notice what was so frightening to the adults around her. Occasionally, she would close her eyes for a moment then start reading her book again. Someone asked the child if she was not worried or afraid because of the storm. She calmly replied, "No, because my daddy's the pilot, and he's taking me home."

We may face many storms on our Life Journey and may be in the midst of some rather heavy turbulence right now at this season of life. This is the time to remember: God is the pilot and he is taking his children home.

A few years ago, I returned to Madison, Indiana for

the funeral of a very special friend. My husband had started a church plant there many years before and that beautiful little river town was home for my family for nine years.

Betty attended the church and became one of those life friends that you might not see for months, or even years, and yet be able to pick up right where you left off when you got together again. She owned the local flower shop in downtown Madison and was one of those calm, collected people who did a great job in everything she did.

There was no advance warning of her death. She simply went to sleep one night on earth and woke the next morning in heaven. But her organizational skills did not end that night. Even in her death, she had a plan for her final arrangements. My son was the preacher for the service, and she wanted the three local funeral directors with whom she had worked for many years to be in charge of her burial plans. She listed all three and gave the specifics of what each was to do. Now the problem was that the three did not always see eye to eye with each other. Betty knew that and even from the grave, she set about to fix things.

After the committal, everyone thought the service was over, but her daughter announced that there was one more item to be take care of. She then produced a hatchet. Yes, a hatchet! This was given to the three undertakers and the word was, "It's time to bury the hatchet." And they did. That was so like Betty. She had learned confidence and contentment and she wanted to pass along these gifts to her friends.

When I was a little girl, I loved to come into church early and run to the front row of the sanctuary. I would come and sit beside a very elderly lady sitting there and place my hand on hers. She would take my little hand and feel it gently and then exclaim with pleasure, "Why! This is my Anne." Miss Brizee was blind, and it fascinated me that she could know who I was. I loved that special time with her. She was always the same, contented and happy in spite of her disability, always ready to give love and precious thoughts to little ones. I do not remember much about her family, except that her sister brought her to church and came back for her when the service was finished. I do know that her joyful spirit, even though she was blind, was a great comfort to a little girl and a very precious memory. Miss Brizee was a living example of 1 Thessalonians 5:18, "Give thanks in all circumstances; for this is God's will for you in Christ Jesus."

We never know what tomorrow holds. A caregiver recently spoke of the sudden change in the one for whom she was caring. He was well and capable one day and suddenly was hit by a stroke which left him incapacitated and confused. The message we must learn is to live one day at a time, grateful and trusting that our sovereign God has it all under control. He knows each heartache and pain we feel, and he cares. And he especially knows and cares about our grief in losing a loved one at this season of life.

I stood at the cemetery alone one day

I had come to a tombstone just to pray

I was sad and lonely and my heart was sore

But God looked down and my joy was restored.

Feeling his love, my heart was content

The deep gloom I felt was quickly spent.

To know God holds my years and my days,

Gives a glorious peace filling my heart with his praise.

God knows my life span, he has planned it all out.

His Word give me comfort – I will not doubt.

I'll be joining my loved one by God's loving grace

As together we reach our heavenly place.

- Truey Anne Sterneman

Action plan for group study

On note paper describe in a few sentences

a time in your life when you were afraid.

How was your problem solved?

The Apostle Paul: Witnessing His Life of Confidence and Contentment

The following was found in a fortune cookie:

The efficient man gets the job done right.
The effective man gets the right job done.

It must be that God knew who would get the right job done when he brought Paul into the fellowship of believers. Paul's story in the New Testament is certainly a marvelous example of God's plan for the people he has created!

Paul was climbing the "Religious Leader" ladder big time. Indeed, his name had become a household word of terror for the Christians living in the days following Jesus' death and resurrection. Paul was chasing them down mercilessly and dragging them off to prison. And he had papers giving him that permission! The established religious community and leaders were so intent on wiping out the new Christian faith they authorized Saul to do all he could to bring down this growing body of believers. Saul was meticulously following their plan. And then . . . . God!

The story unfolds in Acts where Saul was the hate-filled accuser who became the love-filled Paul, the apostle. This action-packed story is found in Acts 9:1-19. And that account is only the beginning. Paul's name change from the Jewish Saul to the Roman Paul is mentioned in Acts 13:9, "But Saul, who was also called Paul," is significant because God called him to be missionary to the Gentiles, or to non-Jews.

From day one of Paul's new life journey as a follower of Christ, his life was filled with incredible accounts of shipwrecks, stonings, being left for dead, beatings, as well as multiple jail terms. Paul is known for his missionary journeys and the accounts of leading people to Christ. But his major contributions were the New Testament books he wrote. He is responsible for writing thirteen of the twenty-seven books found in the New Testament. Paul gives insightful advice on church administration and correction for those who were out of line. A great deal of wise advice and encouragement for the Christian life is found in the Pauline Epistles.

Paul suffered a great deal from his former mentors in his determined advance of the gospel. However, this brave apostle accepted all the harsh treatment and periods of loneliness because he was looking for the blessed hope of heaven and meeting Jesus face to face. Paul had a wonderful way of accepting whatever came to him. Even in the prison after he and his traveling companion, Silas, were so brutally beaten, they were able to sing praises to God. Now that is a picture of confidence and contentment. These men knew that God is sovereign and that he had a plan.

Paul left great words of wisdom in his epistles. The prison epistles, Ephesians, Philippians, Colossians and Philemon, were written when Paul was imprisoned in Rome. When he was released, he was able to make more missionary journeys and after his faithful service to God, he wrote his last letter to his dear young friend Timothy. He was then again imprisoned for his faith and waiting for his inevitable execution. He was most likely lonely and feeling the heartbreak of leaving those dear to him. We read in 2 Timothy 4:16-17, "At my first defense, no one came to my support, but everyone deserted me. May it not be held against them. But the Lord stood at my side and gave me strength, so that through me the message might be fully proclaimed, and all the Gentiles might hear it."

Eternity will bring great rewards to those who are faithful. God understands our sorrow and he will bring confidence and contentment to our lives.

THOUGHT QUESTIONS:

1. How was Paul prepared for the work God gave to him?

2. Can you see how quickly your supporters can turn away? How is that illustrated in Paul's story?

3. What part of Paul's Life Journey especially has an impact on your life?

4. Using his imprisonment to write encouraging words to others shows Paul's characteristics of confidence and contentment. How does this encourage you to be confident and content?

Keeping on action:

Live both for the moment and for the glory of God. That is what Paul did. No matter what life (or his enemies) dished out, Paul learned to use it for God's glory. We, too, can serve God, even when the way is cluttered with problems. Then, when we can no longer actively serve, we can always pray for others.

LESSON 7

❖❖❖❖❖
---

*Enduring and Encouraging
Faith as Exhibited by Joseph*

Blessed is the one who perseveres under trial

because, having stood the test,

that person will receive the crown of life

that the Lord has promised to

those who love him.

James 1:12

Change happens. No one is more aware of that fact than senior citizens. Many have lived with a lot of changes throughout their lives. A retired military wife told me of moving so often it made my head spin! Some others stay put and only experience changes as they watch neighbors move in and out. In our golden years, we can expect changes. We are encouraged to be ready so that with God's help we can embrace whatever comes our way. One dear friend left her beautiful lake home for a small apartment in an assisted living facility. She chose to adapt and now enjoys many close friends and activities. Another close family member had to be moved into a memory care facility because of the disease which was contorting his mind. Here again, a family was faced with challenges and life changes.

In 1911, W.B. Stevens must have had some questions about changes when he wrote the song, "Farther Along." The first line could be the song on our lips as we face this season of life: "Tempted and tried, we're oft made to wonder, why it should be thus all the day long." However, the chorus gives bright hope for the future: "Farther along we'll know more about it. Farther along we'll understand why; cheer up, my brother, live in the sunshine. We'll understand it all by and by."

Certainly, Joni Erickson Tada had major questions about her future when a diving accident changed her life permanently, leaving her a quadriplegic at eighteen years of age. Now in her senior years, Joni can look back at a life journey of helping and encouraging other people with disabilities to live in the sunshine.

Recently I watched some on-line videos of a man born with phocomelia, a rare birth defect that causes a baby to be born with missing limbs. Nick Vujicic was born in Australia in the early eighties with *all* his limbs missing except for one tiny foot. The prognosis was that he would be confined to a life in a wheelchair. However, this amazing man swims, skis, skydives and brings hope to millions of people worldwide. He has a double major in accounting and financial planning and is the CEO of two businesses, traveling thousands of miles yearly. Nick is a motivational speaker and encourages all age groups to live life to its full potential. Nick lives in Southern California with his beautiful wife and four children.

Nick was encouraged by his parents from birth to never give into the "why me" pity party. He early made the choice to accept how God made him. Among his several books is *The Power of Unstoppable Faith*. Nick's trust in God has been the mainstay of his faith and courage. He lives by the maxim, "until you try, you don't know what you can't do."

That is good advice for seniors as we face the challenges of the golden years. When my husband and I moved from our very large bed and breakfast home into a small condominium we were constantly faced with decisions. Even after huge sales and down-sizing, we still had more stuff than we needed. Eventually, however, everything found a place, and we learned to love our new home. That change was best for our new season of life.

The book, *A Good Old* Age, by Derek Prime has some great advice for people facing age-related changes. This book is an A to Z list of priorities for the golden years. Addressing old age directly, the author moves through the alphabet with Attitude for A and Zeal for Z and presents some amazing insights for older adults. His advice is to accept our aging years and the life God daily gives us.

As we move through our golden years, many make their final wishes known. Some make wills and even arrange for and prepay their final expenses. My son, a pastor, likes to have his parishioners list what they would like to have in their memorial service such as favorite scriptures or hymns and any other notes. These last wishes are kept on file in his office until they are needed and are very comforting to the family. In a recent message, he summarized his words on aging with the old saying: "Today is the first day of the rest of your life." Wow, that was an "aha" moment for me! Today is the first day of the rest of my life and I want to live it well. May these days be full of enduring and encouraging faith for all of us.

Embracing life changes is encouraged by the amazing promise we find in Joshua 1:9: "Have I not commanded you? Be strong and courageous. Do not be afraid; do not be discouraged, for the Lord your God will be with you wherever you go."

Action plan for group study

On sticky notes, list some of the changes you
have noticed in these latter years. How have
they challenged and changed your life?

Joseph: His Enduring and Encouraging Faith

Recently, I saw a funny little plaque which read:

Jesus loves you,

But I'm His Favorite!

In speaking to his eleven brothers, Joseph could have
rephrased this to: "Dad loves you, but I'm his favorite."
Partiality usually leads to discord in families and it was
no different with Jacob's family. Jacob's preferential
treatment of his eleventh son, Joseph, was evident to
all. Even Benjamin, Joseph's younger full brother did
not hold the same place in Jacob's heart. Joseph wore
a beautiful coat of many colors which Jacob had given

him. This garment was a constant reminder to all the brothers of where their father's affections were.

Genesis 37:3-4 gives this introduction to the story: "Now Israel (Jacob) loved Joseph more than any of his other sons, because he had been born to him in his old age; and he made an ornate robe for him. When his brothers saw that their father loved him more than any of them, they hated him and could not speak a kind word to him."

The brothers' jealous rage only grew when Joseph added fuel to the fire by telling of the dreams he had. Dreams showing family members bowing down to him. This seemed to be more than his older brothers could handle, and they plotted to kill him when he came to them in the fields. They grabbed him and tore his coat from him. Then they threw him into a pit, thinking this would be a great way to permanently get rid of their odious little brother. However, some Midianite merchants passed by on their way to Egypt, and the brothers sold him into slavery instead of committing murder.

Life in Egypt was a big change for Jacob's favored and petted son! The account of this story in Genesis is a record of God's plan for a boy and for a nation. A sense of God's presence went before Joseph, and through a series of marvelous events, he was given a high position in the land of Egypt, second in power only to Pharaoh himself. This story of God's amazing plan to save his people is told in detail in the book of Genesis chapters 37 to 50. Here we can see how Joseph accepted what God sent his way. He went from being a beloved son to a slave in Potiphar's house. Then, because of his ethical trustworthiness, he was lied about and sent to prison. Even there he endured, holding firmly onto his faith and encouraging other prisoners. From prison, God took Joseph to the palace and a leadership position in the kingdom where he established a program that kept Egypt and his own family back home in Israel from starvation.

God can work through obedient lives. He can meet us in the problem pits of life and bring us into the joy of his presence. God will be with us in our life journey and use us to encourage others through the presence of his Holy Spirit when we put him in control of our lives.

THOUGHT QUESTIONS:

1. Why is partiality in families bad for everyone? Another classic example of favoritism in families is recorded in the book of Genesis. Here, again, we see how preferential treatment can bring destruction to families. Comparing Joseph's "favorite son" status and the favoritism Rebecca and Isaac displayed between their twin sons Jacob and Esau, gives much insight into the importance of loving each child equally.

2. How do you think Joseph felt when his brothers hated him and wanted him dead? How do you think the brothers felt when Joseph forgave them?

3. God allowed Joseph to be taken away from Jacob. How hard is it to lose dear ones?

4. Do you think Joseph realized that his problems were part of God's divine plan for his life?

5. I have always wondered how Potiphar's wife reacted to the news that the one she sought to seduce and lied about, became Pharaoh's top official.

Keeping on action:

Joseph's life is a great example of living God's plan for our lives. Read the account in Genesis 37–50. What the world dished out, God used for Joseph's good. It may be farther along that we understand the hardships we are enduring now. Remember we live in a "fallen world." Keep praising God and trusting him even when you do not understand the road you are traveling. And take a look at the "i" in Derek Prime's little book, *A Good Old Age*. The letter "i" is for intercession.

LESSON 8

Summary – *Everyone has a Life Story: Consider Daniel, the Prayer Warrior*

> **Rejoice in the Lord always. I will say it again: Rejoice! Let your gentleness be evident to all. The Lord is near. Do not be anxious about anything, but in every situation, by prayer and petition, with thanksgiving, present your requests to God.**
>
> **Philippians 4:4-6**

Signatures are an important part of everyone's life. We write our name many times in the course of our life journey. What is a signature worth? George Washington signed the Acts of Congress and that signature is now worth $9.8 million. Abraham Lincoln signed the Emancipation Proclamation and this signature is currently worth $3.7 million.

Our signatures are important because they identify our writing. However, it is that little line between our birth and death dates on our tombstone that is far more important. That line represents how we lived our life story. Many people journal and leave a record of their history and events that filled their journey through life. These journals may become special treasures for the family.

Sarah Young is a devotional writer. Her life story is told in her devotional books which are widely read and enjoyed worldwide. These books come from personal reflections in Bible reading, praying and journaling. In her devotional books, she uses Scripture to give messages of advice from Jesus to readers who are finding their way through the journey of life. Just today, as I was sorrowing about some current happenings in our country, I was blessed by this nugget of wisdom written by Mrs. Young in words such as Jesus might have spoken: ". . . As you trudge through the sludge of this fallen world, keep your mind in Heavenly places with Me. Then the Light of My Presence shines on you, giving peace and joy that circumstances cannot touch."

Even with a good choice of trusting God, it is natural to be concerned about the problems we face, especially the ones that aging brings. Physical challenges cause us to contemplate our days on earth. What more does God want us to accomplish? Psalm 90:12 instructs us to ". . . number our days, that we may gain a heart of wisdom." George Whitfield, minister to the Colonies said, "We are immortal until our work on earth is done." So be intentional about choices – make good ones.

It is good to focus on the blessings. Being positive is a good choice with which to start our day. A little anecdote from A.A. Milne causes us to smile but has great impact. In this little "Pooh clip," Winnie is asking what day it is. Piglet answers that it is today, to which Winnie the Pooh responds that today is his favorite day!

We could use the same positive attitude to set the tone for our days. My mother used to say: "Each day is a gift." Those are words of wisdom, but we might find days when our body determines how that gift will open and how it will be spent. Also, there are days when an afternoon nap is sufficient; other days, however, we need more. We just have to listen to our body and follow directions. No matter what, start your day with prayer and today just might be your favorite day. Our decision is to choose carefully and prayerfully how we will face each day. As we already know, happiness is based on happenings. But joy comes from having a close relationship with God. I love to hear stories of people from the past and how they lived their lives. Everyone has a story!

Harley DeLeurere served God for many years until a stroke ended his public ministry. He was a bi-vocational pastor for most of his pastoral years, working for the railroad in a second job. Both of Harley's jobs gave him much personal satisfaction. Harley was always the same, cheerful and caring, a "what you sees is what you gets" type of person. He never put on a false front. It was always a blessing to visit Harley and his family when my husband and I attended the Hendricks church, part of my husband's conference circuit.

One of Harley's most endearing attributes was that he genuinely loved people. No matter who he met or what their position in life, Harley always had time to stop and listen to people. Then he would tell them that Jesus loved them. No one knew the extent of the wide circle of friends Harley gathered during his life. Certainly no one expected the huge turnout for his funeral in such a tiny mountain town. Hendricks, WV has a population of under 300 people and yet people came from all over to pay their final respects to this dear man. We waited in the viewing line for close to an hour. Some people stood in line for three hours just to honor this man who was interested in people and helping them solve their problems and build their relationship to God.

My mother, Truey Johnston-Cooper, also lived a great story in her small town of Spencerport, NY. She was raised for most of her childhood in a children's home, where her hearing disability set her apart as a problem child. Mom loved to tell us stories of her growing up years. She would tell us about her life at the home and of the punishment meted out to the bad kids. My siblings and I cringed at the story of the terrible beatings the matron's two little favorites received when they tried to do a good deed for her.

The matron was on her day off and the two girls decided to exchange her old straw mat for a nice clean one. They worked hard at this labor of love, burning the old mattress and lugging up a fresh clean mat to her room. The thing they did not know was that the old mattress was the matron's "bank" and held her life savings.

Mom left the home when she was fourteen. At sixteen, she married my father. Their marriage lasted for fifty-five years until my father's death in 1981. Seven children were born into the Johnston family. These children were mom's treasures, and she gave us the love she never knew. She became a legend both to her friends and her church family. She was a great storyteller and rejoiced when a visiting evangelist told her, "Truey, you were just a little nobody, and God made someone special out of you." At 101 years, she was given her heavenly send-off before a crowd of about 250 people. Her favorite saying was "I love you and Jesus loves you better." In fact, her tombstone in Sacketts Harbor, NY is inscribed with the words: "Jesus Loves You."

In these golden years, we have time to sit back and enjoy life. Some do this by gardening and growing flowers, and this can be a delightful task to fill one's days. Others find puzzles or reading books or just hanging out with friends to be enjoyable ways to fill their days. The thing is, do something you like to do, have fun and be cheerful. There is the story of one older lady who plays dominoes with her husband. It was a game they had enjoyed for years calling it their "Alzheimer's medicine." Only now, she has to play both racks because her husband has preceded her into the heavenly realms. Short-term memory problems really help here, she says. His rack often wins, and it gives her a sense of his nearness and pleasant memories.

Then, best of all, in these golden years, we have more time to pray and wait upon God. We have a choice as to how our life is spent. In 1855, Joseph Scriven wrote the beloved hymn, *What a Friend We Have in Jesus*. This song was written after several personal tragedies. Here are a few lines that could speak to us in this season of life: "What a friend we have in Jesus, all our sins and griefs to bear! What a privilege to carry everything to God in prayer!"

Mr. Scriven made a good choice when he led us to prayer. God cares and he understands. Make it a point to be intentional about encouraging someone every day. Making others happy brings joy to the giver as well as the receiver.

Action plan for group study

Consider taking a 3-hole notebook with twelve dividers. Behind each divider place at least thirty-one sheets of note paper, numbering the sheets according to the days in the month. In just a few lines, list your day's events. Some people can get three to four years on such a page. Each night when you record the day's events, you can catch a glimpse of what you were doing last year and the years before. This is an easy way to track one's life journey.

Daniel, the Prayer Warrior: A Story of a Man Dedicated to God and the Power of Prayer

Only one life, yes only one,

Now let me say, "Thy will be done."

And when at last I'll hear the call,

I know I'll say "'twas worth it all,"

Only one life, 'Twill soon be past,

Only what's done for Christ will last.

These words, penned by the English missionary, C. T. Studd, could have been written by the Prophet Daniel, who was a great Old Testament hero. Daniel's life was spent worshiping and obeying God, and God honored him in many ways for his unswerving obedience.

The book of Daniel records many awesome events such as Daniel's ability to interpret dreams, the three men in the fiery furnace, the captivating story of Daniel in the lion's den and his incredible angelic delivery. Also, most students of Bible prophecy would say that they look to the book of Daniel to interpret how they see the future unfold.

Daniel's story begins with the first captivity of God's people when they were carried off to Babylon in 1607 BC for disobedience and turning from God. Daniel and his three friends were young, handsome, and bright Jewish boys. They soon caught the attention of the king, and he had the boys brought to a place where they could be trained in Babylonian ways and leadership. All four boys moved up the success ladder with Daniel becoming the chief minister at Nebuchadnezzar's royal palace.

When troubles came to Daniel, he first turned to prayer. We read in Daniel 2:17-19: "Then Daniel returned to his house and explained the matter to his friends Hananiah, Mishael and Azariah. He urged them to plead for mercy from the God of heaven concerning this mystery, so that he and his friends might not be executed with the rest of the wise men of Babylon. During the night the mystery was revealed to Daniel in a vision. Then Daniel praised the God of heaven."

Daniel lived such an exemplary life before God that when Daniel's enemies looked for something to "get him on," they could find nothing. The only thing they could find was his faithfulness to prayer. This they used to try to destroy him, creating a document which they had the king sign. This imperial document forbade people from praying to the God of heaven. Daniel 6:10 records Daniel's reaction. "Now when Daniel learned that the decree had been published, he went home to his upstairs room where the windows opened toward Jerusalem. Three times a day he got down on his knees and prayed, giving thanks to his God, just as he had done before."

Prayer was Daniel's secret weapon and he was faithful to God even when threatened with death. The Bible records the gripping climax to this event: Daniel was set free and his jealous enemies were punished. Such undeniable heavenly intervention underscores the truth that God is pleased when we pray!

Daniel's thrilling life story gives encouragement to all who put their trust in God. He outlived Nebuchadnezzar and finished his life journey in Babylon in his nineties.

THOUGHT QUESTIONS:

1. Daniel was just a teenager when he was taken as a slave to Babylon. What do you think he was feeling when he was carried away?

2. Daniel's desire to keep living by God's standards put him in jeopardy. How do you think he was able to stand against the rules and regulations which were forced upon him? Remember, he was very young.

3. How would we react to being thrown to the lions for praying to our God?

4. Why is prayer so important?

Keeping on action:

Throughout our study, emphasis has been placed on choices and prayer. Now, as we live out our senior years, prayer is the last gift we can give to our loved ones. Never underestimate the power of prayer and our God who answers by his sovereign grace. Keep on living for God. Do not grow old. Choose to live your life victoriously right to the end no matter what hard issues come your way. May your faithful service be an offering to God. Eternity waits and we look forward to those words: "Well done, good and faithful servant."

RECOMMENDED BOOKS ON GROWING OLDER

Bright, Bill. *The Journey Home, Finishing with Joy.* Nashville: Thomas Nelson Publishers, 2003.

Crosby, Fanny. *Fanny Crosby's Life Story, by Herself.* New York: EveryWhere Publishing Company, 1903.

Dunlop, John. *Finishing Well to the Glory of God: Strategies from a Christian Physician.* Wheaton: Crossway, 2011.

Prime, Derek. *A Good Old Age from A to Z.* Leyland, England: 10Publishing, 2017.

Rivers, Francine. *Unashamed.* Carol Stream, IL: Tyndale, 2000.

Vujicic, Nick. *The Power of Unstoppable Faith*. New York: Crown Publishing Group, 2014.

Young, Sarah. *Jesus Calling: Enjoying Peace in His Presence*. Nashville: Thomas Nelson Publishers, 2004, 2011.

Story Notes for

_____

Birth - I was born in (place):

_____

_____

Childhood - (0-14) Tell of a childhood experience:

_____

_____

_____

Teen & young adult (15-25) - School and beyond memories:

_____

_____

_____

Mid-life (25-64) - Family and work thoughts:

_____

_____

_____

The Now Years (65+) - The golden years:

_____

_____

_____

What is your biggest joy?

_____

_____

_____

What is your biggest problem/need?

_____

_____

_____

How can you live for Jesus now to ensure that you will hear that blessed: "Well done, good and faithful servant." when you get to heaven?

_____

_____

_____

Printed in the United States
By Bookmasters